A Simplified Gu[ide to] Church Websites. Purpose, Planning, and Presentation

It's late 2015 as I write about website design and development for the first time. The purpose of this book is to share the knowledge and techniques that I have learned in a decade of self-taught web design. That's why I know anyone can use the information I am presenting. However, it is also why I know that I cannot call it a comprehensive guide, since I have somewhat limited experience as a freelance web designer. Since my goal is usually to build websites fast so that I can USE them, my tips and tricks are meant to free you to build rather than drown you in theory.

The basic outline of the book is to argue for a website, instruct on how to build a page from top to bottom, and then suggest pages and add-ons for an effective website. While my perspective is that of someone who builds using a Content Management System and templates, I attempt to take other views into account, while still focusing on the fastest and easiest way to get the job done.

While the target audience for this book would be church staff or decision-makers, it can certainly be used by volunteers looking to help out with the church's web presence. Actually, I could see a talented high school student taking these ideas and forming a church website design business. With some practice, anyone can learn to build a modern, mobile-friendly website in less than a week. If you already have a website that just needs some tweaking, this book offers several easy methods for finishing sometimes complicated tasks. If nothing else, it shows you that it CAN be done, even if it means hiring someone to help out.

A lot of what I write could have been written a decade ago and still be relevant today, which means much of this guide will likely stay relevant as the internet continues to change. That said, I just received an order from a client who wants a new design after about a year. My goal is to help you create a website that can stand the test of time in most ways, even if you change some parts of it in a year or less. Some of the sites I built nearly a decade ago are still just as useful today, even if they've needed some design upgrades. If you start out smart or make some of the changes I suggest, your website will be better for a longer time. In addition, you'll understand the why and how of making some of the changes you will eventually need, even the ones that have yet to be imagined.

Contents

Why Does Our Church Need a Website?

You've probably read the stats about how a percentage of people meet their future spouses online or shop online. Wouldn't it make sense that the same people shop for their future churches, schools, and child cares online? You might claim you don't need a website because most of your membership is aging, but what if the fact that your website is aging plays a role in why your membership is aging? According to a survey from Search Engine Watch (and reposted on many sites), 75% of people are more likely to return to a site if it works well on a mobile phone, while 61% quickly leave a site that is not mobile-friendly. Young, vibrant people with children and short attention spans want you to have a website that is modern and mobile-friendly. The mega-church down the road has one. The school district in town has one. The chain child care facility across town has one. Yes, you DO need a website, and you DO need it to be modern, mobile-friendly, and done quickly.

So you do need a website, but all the salesmen out there know you need one, and that's where it gets tricky. Many churches overdesign and overpay in the hopes that staff or volunteers will find time to keep the website updated, buying expensive upsell items in the process. Other churches try to develop a website of their own, not realizing the time-commitment involved in simply getting a few pages online and looking respectable. The purpose of this guide is to discuss why the website is needed and how to create it most effectively. It's not an exhaustive guide as it's meant to be something a church staff member or volunteer could use. However, I will attempt to cover most of the basics and some of the intricate details of creating an effective, modern, user-friendly website.

Will a Website Make Our Church Grow?

The short answer is, "No." There are web designers and marketers out there who like to promise a lot. The website will not grow the church. However, it can help. More importantly, the CONTENT on the website and how it relates to your church home CAN grow your church. Let's take a look at the main factors for growth in Church of England churches. With all kinds of data, researchers figured that these were the most important factors in growing a church:

- Good leadership
- A clear mission and purpose
- Willingness to self-reflect, to change and adapt according to context
- Involvement of lay members
- Being intentional in prioritising growth
- Being intentional in chosen style of worship
- Being intentional in nurturing disciples

http://www.churchgrowthresearch.org.uk/UserFiles/File/Reports/FromAnecdoteToEvidence1.0.pdf

These factors can all be presented or promoted on a website, in articles or using a calendar. However, you might notice that "a good website" is not on the list. You can certainly argue that a modern, mobile-friendly, and constantly updated website would be an obvious step for these growing churches, and it more than likely is, but it's not the single magic bullet that will save all churches. In fact, it's probably more of a reflection of what's going on in the church rather than a driving force. If a church is serious about growth, involvement, being intentional, and having a clear mission, it would almost have to be on the website. On the other hand, a poorly-designed and maintained website is not necessarily an indicator of failing church, but one can assume it's a church that probably lacks at least some of the above attributes (or a church that absolutely loves using a lot of paper).

From the book *Autopsy of a Deceased Church*, a few of the chapter titles about reasons for churches dying include:

- The Past is the Hero
- The Church Refused to Look Like the Community
- The Great Commission Becomes the Great Omission
- The Church Rarely Prayed Together
- The Church Had No Clear Purpose

These Chapters represent nearly half the book. Again, the author does not say that a lackluster website will kill a church, but all of the listed items can be addressed using a website. For example, a History page is good, but an embedded Google Calendar is better. Community organizations are building mobile-friendly websites. A good website can help you reach out to others. A prayer at church is good, but members who can't make it to church might want to see those same prayers online. The church website is the perfect place to post your church's purpose and goals for all to see. A website may not make your church great, but a great church will make a website that reaches out to current and new members.

But Nobody Has Complained About Our Current Website

Your church members probably don't mind your outdated website, just like they might not mind the outdated crying room or ministry contact list. At least the members who don't care won't mind. And the members who never officially become members don't mind, either. If you're involved with or work for a church, you have a lot on your plate. The design of the website might seem like something you can wait on. It's not.

The reason nobody mentions the website is because it's not impressive. If the awe-inspiring cathedrals in Europe were designed like office buildings, would we tour them? People who are virtually touring your church for the first time or checking in to see what's going on want to see more than framed boxes. They want to see your vibrant church at its best. And on a mobile device. If you are reading this right now, more than likely your church website needs to be updated, probably in a major way. People aren't talking about it because most of them don't realize how outdated your site has become. However, just because the orange countertops in someone's kitchen still function does not mean that's what makes sense. And just as no one will come into that kitchen and tell the owner how bad the countertops look, most people are not going to tell you that a website redesign is in order. They just won't show up to worship with you or send their kids to your school.

(image) Some examples of LCMS websites in 2015 partying like it's 1999.

What Kind of Website Works Best?

In this section, I will discuss some of the frameworks for modern websites.

CMS

Simply put, you need a Content Management System (CMS). Even if most of your site is made up of static content, a CMS just works better for most tasks, including being able to turn pages into blogs, add components, and update the site to new standards, not to mention the ability to update the site from anywhere. The big three CMS options as of 2015 are WordPress, Drupal, and Joomla. You might hear about Ruby on Rails or Concrete 5, or a few dozen other CMS options, but they're all fairly similar. Your web developer will like one more than the others. Some of these web developers will try to make it appear as if the CMS they use is their own, but normally it is a paid or free CMS script. You pay for implementation of a free script, like WordPress, but it can be very worth the money, since your alternative would be to figure it all out yourself. Of course, you can order a much more complicated or fully-custom website for a lot more money, though it's rarely worth the extra amount. Why? Think of it this way: a lot of people pay a little bit for templates and add-ons when they use Open Source CMS scripts, but YOU alone pay a lot if you hire a custom web developer. For example, if you want a custom photo animation, a firm might charge $1000 to create it. However, you can probably get an add-on to a Joomla site for $1, since that developer is looking to sell it 1,000 times at $1 each. Maybe 10,000.

https://en.wikipedia.org/wiki/List_of_content_management_systems

I use Joomla CMS with Rockettheme Templates. I have shifted to the Gantry 5 system for Rockettheme. If you are just getting into designing your own site, I'd recommend trying your hand at the newest version of a CMS and its add-ons, since it will be old in a hurry, and you might as well learn the newest version when you can. I made the mistake, while teaching, of letting my own websites fall behind the times a bit. This was partially due to the fact that my host made it difficult to upgrade, which is really another issue with running your own CMS: hosts will promise an easy system to create and update, but they often do not provide the latest framework for you to do so (PHP, MySQL, JavaScript, etc.) I had my host move my sites to a newer server in order to continue using its services, but most weekend website warriors might not even know to ask, giving up before they can get started.

"Free" or Monthly Fee Sites

Another way to build your new site is to use a CMS tied into a host, building it yourself. These hosts try to make it simple with drag and drop functionality. However, these systems are not any easier than a well-built site using any other CMS by a web designer. You just save the initial design costs, paying those fees to staff members as they learn. These hosts will often allow you to have a free website as a subdomain, all the while encouraging you to upgrade to a paid version. This option is much cheaper than fully-custom-built sites, and it's also cheaper than hiring a freelancer, but the companies you will be dealing with make their money off upselling other services. This option can be economical, but be careful. Also, you DO NOT want your main church domain to be a subdomain of any sort, so totally free is not a good option. These sites look fine and work well. Just make sure you're prepared to learn how to use them, and be sure to understand what the price options include. One problem that I learned about in my research is that if you have these companies create your Facebook, Google+, or other related pages, they OWN those pages, not letting you take ownership--just another way they try to keep you paying the monthly fees. Here's a list of sites I've tried out for free just to see what they offer: WordPress, Weebly, Yola, Wix, Sharefaith, and more. Honestly, they are all very similar and all can be learned. If you go with one of these, expect to learn a lot and pay something. You can also expect your technical assistance to be overseas with many of these hosted website companies.

Another free option is Google Sites, which requires a steep learning curve and has almost no add-ons, which seems to indicate these sites are not really supported by Google. So far,

I have not seen mobile-friendly versions of these sites, either. However, with a limited budget, they provide a great way of integrating Google Drive with a serviceable website, and maybe Google will put money into upgrading or promoting these sites in the future, though it looks like the company is more focused on design platforms for Android-only as of 2015.

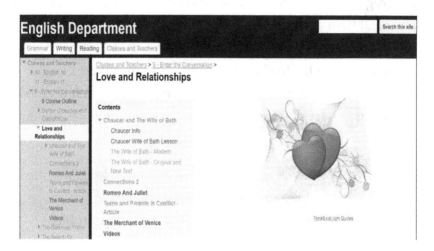

(image) A Google Site I created for my classroom teaching.

Volunteer

Another kind of website you can get is the volunteer website. You have good people at your church. Some of them want to help with the website. I did at my church many years ago. The problem was that volunteers don't make good employees. Since I was teaching, I didn't want to build the new site when it was needed because I was teaching a new class at school. Another church member liked it the way it was. A third "volunteer" said she'd build it for free, only to bill the church thousands later on to "feed" her artist at her marketing company.

Needless to say, there were hard feelings. One member left the church. The one who built the site is seen by some members as a rip-off artist, and I felt like my talents and opinions were wasted. The stories I've heard from other congregations are often similar: volunteers who are more technical than aesthetic; volunteers who never actually do the work; volunteers who accidentally destroy entire sites, volunteers who try to charge because it's hard work. I've heard it all and seen the results. The truth is that even if your volunteer is very good and very giving, something can still go wrong.

You WANT to have great volunteers willing to keep the site maintained, but I know from experience that having volunteers create the initial site is often more of a problem than you can imagine. Ask for volunteers to create artwork for the site, write content, and keep it fresh, but getting tied into a volunteer may not be the wisest choice. That said, it can work well. If your volunteer is a freelancer who has a portfolio and some free time, give it a shot, but if it's someone just looking to learn how to do something new, be afraid.

Clunky

Yes, I forgot to mention non-websites like Facebook or Google+. And clunky sites like asp.net. They are barely worth mentioning, except for that someone at some point will tell you they are a good idea. Let's start with asp.net, which is a CMS created by Microsoft in order to employ people with six-figure salaries, since those are the people you will need to help you figure it out. My wife learned how to use Joomla (most of it) in a weekend, and it takes maybe a week to master most aspects of many of the CMSes you can use, but I cannot make heads or tails of asp.net, and I think there are plenty of wealthy people who like it that way. I once read a forum post wherein an asp developer was looking for all the reasons he could use to sell a company on his platform instead of Joomla, and fellow asp developers couldn't give him anything to use, until a Joomla developer stepped in and said there was nothing. There might be some argument for security issues, since hackers (mostly from China) will try to get into your CMS. Other clunky sites would include anything built using Dreamweaver or FrontPage from a decade ago, and some churches still have these. Not mobile-friendly, stuck on one computer, old-looking, and a lot more. Basically, while asp.net makes it look like you spent too much on a system meant for Fortune 500 corporations, those older systems make your organizations look amateurish.

Another way to appear to be an amateur organization online is to rely on social media pages as your main websites. The goal is to direct potential members or students to YOUR website, not for you to drive more traffic to the social media sites so that people can get bombarded with paid ads by your competitors. Sure, you can use Facebook, Twitter, photo sites, and YouTube to update people on what you're doing at church, but all the sites should be linked to your main homepage and vice versa, and social media content should be embedded in your site whenever possible. However, I've seen church homepages as Facebook pages, with service times posted way at the bottom of the timeline. You'll have an article about Sunday School snacks right before the week's sermon and no way of searching for that insightful article about why God matters.

(image) Notice the ads on the side of this Facebook church "website."

Some Reasons Why Websites Don't Work

Time Commitment

The number one reason your website is not working like you want and will not work like you want is because you cannot spend endless time updating the site. Tools do exist to make this process easier, but the fact remains that most clients I have worked with have no interest in maintaining a legitimate web presence on their own. They might want a content management system because they've heard it's the way to go, but they really just want a few static pages and a blog, maybe.

The truth is that your site, whether old school, CMS, or a Facebook page is going nowhere without updating.

Depending on the system, this can be done by one person or many individuals, but it needs to get done. There are a few tricks that will be mentioned later on, but adding content to a site is the most important task in having a website anyone cares about.

Too Difficult

A reason for avoiding site updates might include the difficulty in learning the system, especially if employees are responsible for certain sections or pages. It also might not fit into the main role of the employee. For example, when I was teaching, I needed to create assignments and then add them to the site. That's an extra step. However, I saw it as a one-time commitment because the assignment would be there next year. Most paid CMS systems are business solutions adapted to church or school applications. Therefore, the parts might not fit perfectly. Most LMS systems (like Moodle) have a very steep learning curve for the user, and I've seen more neglected sites using these systems than any other.

My idea, and if you're a network administrator, you might be able to figure this out, is to force employees to update the page they're responsible for upon login. You can't go anywhere in the morning until you update your page. Another idea is just allow static content for those who just want that and provide incentives to those who update their pages. Finally, you could hire someone to provide not only the system but also work with the individuals on their pages to at least create a uniform look and feel, whether updated or not.

Websites are often too difficult for the user, as well. A few years back, many prominent sites started getting away from mega menus in order to clean up the main pages. However, navigation gets difficult. Not all menus show up well in tablets or phones, too. I'd say have the huge menus as people with real computers can get where they're going quickly. I would also important main page content with links to currently relevant pages, even if those pages are several years old, like a fundraiser you do every year. You don't need to recreate the page all the time; just bury it in a menu and write about it once a year.

Not a Destination

Even if you have current information, people may not flock to your site. In many cases, churches and schools send our e-newsletters completely separate from the site. People rely on these more than visiting the site, which makes the site irrelevant and the content on the site only an archive. This is especially annoying at my church because I have to login somewhere just to read the e-newsletter, but that somewhere is NOT the official website. Rather, it's some paid service that not only gets all the traffic but also probably is allowed to send out its own emails or throw some ads on its site. A CMS will generally have a free way to send emails out. It can also store emails and profiles, which could save you time over other systems (or could add time).

Other options for driving people to your site would be for photos, videos, or other ways for members to interact in a unique way. We all get many text messages and emails, but seeing a picture of yourself volunteering for church is kind of exciting. You could send out an interesting question that a pastor or principal has answered on the site only. If you are really on a budget but have a little extra time, find out each member's cell phone provider so that you can send free texts out to their phones via email (yes, this works). Conversely, you could opt for refusing to cater to laziness and only put general information on the website. No newsletter or texts or anything, but an updated, relevant website. A combination of these methods is likely the best scenario, which means time and talent.

Not Working on All Devices

Since you're trying to reach everyone with you website, you do need to make it a "responsive" or "mobile-friendly" design. Some web designers have just made this a default skinny design, which still might not show up right in phones, but probably works most of the time. Of course, these fixed thin designs take away from the professional appearance. Some have made these designs just for the mobile version of the site. However, if you're looking at a redesign or upgrade, just go with one responsive template. You can check out responsiveness by simply resizing a site in your browser to look like the dimensions of a phone or tablet. If nothing resizes and it looks awful, you might need some changes. Keep in mind that sales of PCs and even notebooks are no longer the majority of device sales in America, so you need to plan accordingly, but you also have to consider those of us who DO use PCs at home, maybe even on a large screen TV.

Website Advice From Top to Bottom

You might wonder why a web designer wants to help you make your church website better. My wife wondered the same thing, since it's been next to impossible to sell excellent website designs to churches. Will my business really be helped by offering the best advice I have so that churches can go ahead and do it all themselves? Maybe not. Maybe all I will do with this book is provide a decent guide for you to follow, resulting in better church websites and more people showing up at church. Then I'll find another line of work in a better world, and I won't mind much. The other possibility is that you'll see the work needed and figure you might want some help along the way, even if you do understand the general principles. You'll better understand what a web developer can and can't do for you, which will actually make my job easier. Plus, you'll see why you don't need or want high-priced design boutiques or "free" cookie-cutter services, which will also benefit me. The point is that websites are all pretty much the same to some degree, and that's why this book can help you with that $20,000 website you got as a discount from a church member or that free site you set up with your staff.

Since my goal is to help you as much as myself, I will have to be honest in all aspects of this book. That's the difference between me and other web developers. I want to be honest and help you. Therefore, I'm not going to upsell you on services or confuse you with technospeak (if I can help it). The method I will use will be laid out like your webpage, starting with the home page and then working out to other pages and add-ons. I'll finish with some of the extras you might consider or that you might need but don't realize exist.

The Homepage

Most of the important design elements are focused on the main page of a website, so that's where we'll start.

The Favicon

Importance 4/10

Difficulty 7/10 on older sites; 3/10 on many newer sites

A favicon is an icon at the way top of the page. Google has a little "G." Most professional sites have an icon at the top. Favicons are kind of a hassle to create, and you have to remember to name them favicon.ico, as they cannot be jpgs or gifs. Some of the free sites allow you to add a jpg that gets converted, but that's not normally an option. The tricky part comes in with uploading the .ico file to the right place (under the templates folder in Joomla). You can search your type of website to find out where it needs to be, but then the question is whether or not you have access to that location. Probably not if your web developer wants complete control.

Favicons are nice because someone with 50 open tabs can see your site. Plus, when they bookmark the site, the icon shows up in bookmarks instead of a blank image or the image of your CMS (WordPress or Weebly, for example). The favicon is one more way to advertise your brand, but it's not the most important part of a website by any means.

Newer templates make it easier to use a favicon because you can upload any image that's converted and compressed to go in the small box available. One of the "free" website building templates had that as part of the upgrade package, but you can get templates for Joomla or WordPress that offer the same functionality. In fact, the new method is so simple that every site should have a favicon in the near future.

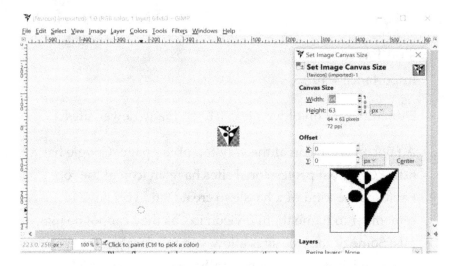

(images) Using GIMP photo editor to create a favicon, which should always be named favicon.ico and saved to the appropriate folder in your file manager (in the template being used in Joomla).

Page Title

Importance 5/10

Difficulty 5/10

Of the pages within your website, page titles are most important on your homepage, as you don't want visitors and search engines to see Home as the main descriptor in the title bar. However, even if that's the case, as long as you have a unique favicon and solid meta tags, people are able to get to your site, and most of them won't really notice what's in the title bar. Most templates will add a title based on the page, so the "History" category page will have the word "History" in the title. You can often select a setting that also adds your site title to the title of each page, either before or after the page title, like this: "History - Luthernet Web Design Services".

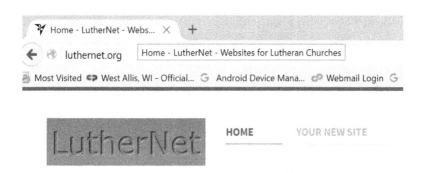

(image) Favicon (Passive Ninja Triangle) and then the page title. It's longer on mouse over.

Site Name and Url

Importance 6/10

Difficulty 3/10

You might not have much of a choice with the site name, since your church already has a name. It's best if you can get the exact, short name of your organization, if it's available. For example, calvary.org is better than calvarylutheran.org is better than calvaryevangelicallutheran.org. If you go by celc instead of Calvary Evangelical Lutheran Church, then see if celc.org is available. At this point in the game, you probably have a site name chosen, so I won't dwell on it too much. If there are two Calvary churches in your town, you might want to make sure your denomination appears right in the site name, but not necessarily in the url. A short, meaningful acronym, combination word, or descriptive word might work, too, especially if all variations of calvarylutheran are taken and you don't want to add your city name to the end of the url. You could use godfun.org or something like that, and then just keep the page title Calvary Evangelical Lutheran Church. You might get some unexpected hits.

Meta Tags and Meta Description

Importance 8/10

Difficulty 5/10

While the content of your site should get folks to your page, Google looks for these tags and description, as well. In my experience, using the meta tags and meta description is important for the main page. You don't really want your description in search results to be some standard CMS description or nothing at all, since it's your one chance to entice new visitors to your site with a nice sentence based on keywords used in the search. Of course, it's even better to have every article published with a descriptive sentence and matching keywords, but that might end up being a lot of work. I'd recommend tags and descriptions on at least the main page and other static pages on a website.

I am going to go ahead and tell you that I am not a Search Engine Optimization (SEO) expert. In fact, an article I wrote many years ago that worked its way to #1 on Google is no longer found at all on Google, and I can't exactly tell why. If I had that knowledge, I'd write a book on just that and sell it for more money than this book. You can hire someone to help with SEO or you can write content and hope that just having it does the trick. While you are competing against other churches, to some extent, it's just not quite the same as a local business, so I'm not going to claim it's totally necessary to optimize your website for SEO. However, using meta tags, meta descriptions, submitting a sitemap to be indexed in Webmaster Tools, and checking your Google Analytics will not hurt.

```
<!DOCTYPE html>
<html lang="en-gb" dir="ltr">

<head>
        <meta name="viewport" content="width=device-width, initial-scale=1.0">
        <meta http-equiv="X-UA-Compatible" content="IE=edge" />

    <base href="http://luthernet.org/" />
    <meta http-equiv="content-type" content="text/html; charset=utf-8" />
    <meta name="keywords" content="church websites, lutheran church websites, lcms web design, wels web design, elca web design, martin luther, protestant church web design, web developer, adlantics web design, wisconsin web design, washington web design, ken berlin, wisconsin, mke web design, Milw." />
    <meta name="description" content="Web Design and Consulting for Lutheran Church, School, and Child Care" />
    <meta name="generator" content="Joomla! - Open Source Content Management" />
    <title>Home - LutherNet - Websites for Lutheran Churches</title>
```

(image) Meta-tags and meta-description in the source code. Click "view source" to see yours.

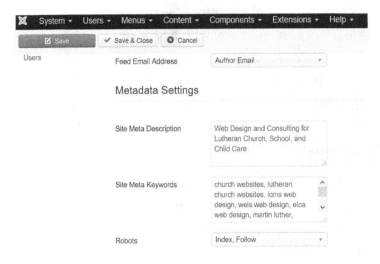

(image) Meta-data in the Joomla admin panel.

Logo

Importance 5/10

Difficulty 5/10

Your logo does not have to be an image that drapes across the entire website, but it should probably be more than the text of your site name. It also doesn't have to have a prominent role at the top of your page, next to the menu, as has become the custom. On one site redesign, I used a brand new logo on the front page, an older logo as the footer, and a third, even older logo, on the contact page. It looked fine that way, but it would have been too much for the eyes to have all three logos across the top of every page. You can get your logo made cheaply by a graphic artist if you need one. If you have one, it can be resized to fit on any website. I try to keep a logo on the front page at least, but the brand recognition with a church and its logo is not as important as with other businesses, since every Christian church shares the same standard logo (the cross). We've added synod logos to church pages, as well, but it seems that no standard for how this is to be presented exists at this time. Images and imagery are important, especially on the front page.

If you're looking for an interesting text logo or to edit images together to create a logo, I'd recommend GIMP, which is an Open Source image editor that works a lot like Photoshop. While it's not the easiest to learn, you can create cool logos with clear backgrounds--it's kind of a trick, actually. Create a logo using the File→ Create→ Logo, select the background (with the move tool) and drag it out of the frame, and then export it as a .png file. You'll be surprised how cool some of these logos look just using the basic settings. You can even make animated .gif files with GIMP. GIMP does take time to learn, so it might be a good school or volunteer project. If you're just looking to try out a logo, use my directions above with maybe a dozen preset logo templates, and you'll find something that works.

(image) Creating a logo in GIMP.

(images) Some examples of logos created using GIMP:

Interchange

Passive Ninja

LutherNet

McNewsy

SITCOM LIFE LESSONS

Sitcom Life Lessons

SATISFAMILY

Green Spin Gifting

Green Spin Gifting

Voucher School

Menu and Mobile Menu

Importance 10/10

Difficulty 8/10

You cannot say everything that's important about your church on a single page. If you have more than one page, you need a menu. While it can be in the form of a top menu, side menu, or even a centered picture menu, it has to exist. Not only is it necessary, but it's also the most difficult part to get right or with which to be satisfied. Many clients will tell their web designers they want 30 menu items (only to use 10). Other clients want it simple: Church and Child Care, but then want news under each, and forms under each, and photos… you get the picture. I will discuss suggested menu items later on, hopefully to create a standard that can help you decide which ones to choose and which ones to lose.

A major issue in creating menu items is that it takes a few steps using a CMS like Joomla or WordPress. There's also a greater chance of messing up a website than in just adding articles, which is why a lot of churches either order too many menu items to start or keep adding articles to the wrong categories.

Right now, you just have to realize that in order for site visitors to get to all those pages you want to create, you will need a menu. As of 2015, it is also imperative to have a separate mobile menu, but not a separate mobile site. Without a mobile menu, the links to pages simply don't work well, which means half of the people looking at your site might be stuck on the main page.

(image) A menu.

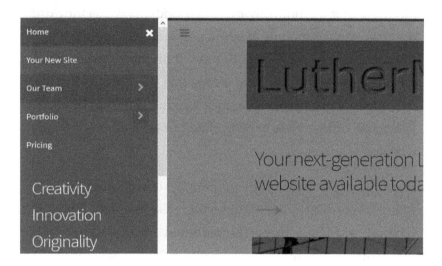

(image) A mobile menu on the same site.

Modern, Mobile-Friendly Design

Importance 10/10

Difficulty 8/10

Actually, this is a good time to mention the most important factor as of right this moment in website design: mobile-friendly (sometimes called responsive) design. This used to be called "fluid" design, and there are probably other terms, as well. The point is that the template, words, and images adjust to the width of the screen. Certain elements can be turned on or off based on screen size, too (like large images or mobile menus). People have embraced mobile technology, and Google is rewarding those who adapt. If your site does not pass Google's mobile-friendly test, it is losing out to other churches, schools, and child care facilities that are mobile-friendly. Simple.

However, getting the page mobile-friendly is not simple. Our old fluid sites are not fully mobile-friendly because they did not have mobile menus. Narrow pages are not mobile-friendly because they are still wider than the 7" screens that have become standard. This means that your professionally-developed, fairly-expensive, nice-looking site from three years ago either needs to be updated or trashed. Let's hope updated.

If you have a Content Management System (CMS) like Joomla, WordPress, or Drupal, you really just need a new template or theme. Sure, you might have to hire someone, but it's mostly connecting the old positions to the new template. However, if you have Joomla 1.0, 1.5, or 2.5, now you're talking about a $500 upgrade to Joomla 3.4, which means a small site might be better off abandoned. Same holds true for major updates of other CMS sites. Anyhow, contact your web developer and ask. We've seen plenty of sites on new versions of WordPress and an older template, and we'd recommend that you ask for a free upgrade in some cases, especially if the site is newer.

If you do not currently have a CMS, that's not necessarily a bad thing. Now is a great time to get one, and you won't have to deal with trying to migrate old CMS to new CMS. Most of them are a lot easier to use than in the past, they have all kinds of add-ons, and most of them update with a few clicks rather than using ftp uploads and database copying of the past. The templates that are available compete with any custom boutique designs, and there are plenty of reputable freelancers waiting for you to find them. All this means your new site could take a lot less time to develop, be easier for you to use, and cost a fraction of what you paid for a site a few years ago.

You could also go the design-it-yourself route (discussed earlier), as these are newer designs that are always mobile-friendly. If you have a few creative team members and hours in the budget to use on learning (and implementing) a new system, these can be the most economical way to build a new site (of course, the hours do add up). To us, after trying out at least 5 of these options, they are very similar to popular CMS designs. You will get confused every now and again. And frustrated. You will question your choice when the site doesn't look like you'd expected and it took you many hours to make it look that way, but you might save $1,000 or more, so it's an option. These companies can sometimes be predatory with setting up other pages or promoting your site with SEO or advertising, so be careful. You also will not be able to take the site elsewhere like with other designs, since it's all housed with them and using their proprietary software for editing. While their sales will be here, their customer service will be in India, but that's not uncommon, and it might be a wonderful opportunity to spread the Word.

What makes design modern is debatable. Every two years, it changes. Not long ago, it was popular to have a huge image with the menu embedded on the image, just after a rotating image next to text. We've seen some church sites with an odd scroll bar on every page to keep it short. Another new one is an image matrix instead of rotating images, maybe with animations, like luthernet.org. We've even seen brand-new designs going back to side menus, so that 8 year-old design of yours might be modern again. You can pick a design you think looks good. Just make sure it's mobile-friendly.

(image) A modern, mobile-friendly website. This one does not have animated images, but that would be an option.

(image) Mobile version of the same site.

Main Images

Importance 8/10

Difficulty 7/10

If a picture is worth a thousand words, then it makes sense to have at least one good image on your homepage. While it's been popular to rotate those images, you can also go more artistic or iconic with one or more vivid images. These can even be random, changing each time someone shows up at the site. The point is that you have at least one image. The more moving parts you try to implement, generally, the more difficult it will be, and you also have to be aware of load times. For example, I've seen homepages with one-minute load times because someone used a full-size, 6mb image. Users will navigate away instead of waiting. However, I've also seen badly pixilated images that end up looking terrible on large screens, so you might have to resize to a bit over 100kb. Images on a homepage is a game of tradeoffs, and those popular image rotators also use bandwidth, so there's a lot to consider. Plus, the larger your image, the further down the viewer might have to scroll to see any content, so that's another consideration, and that's why large images with text appearing on the image are a recently-popular option.

On a more literary note, I often try to create a metaphor with the images I choose for a website. A financial planning site might have a bridge. A site that sells organic essential oils might have plants. A chiropractor's site might have a sunrise. You might want your main images to show your facilities, but church is about a lot more than the buildings. People with smiling faces are good, but abstract ideas also speak to those seeking a church home.

Another area that might be important to you when it comes to images is whether the images can be found in the search engines. You can name an image, give it a description, and add a caption in order to get the search engines to find the image. This can be very useful if you have an image somewhere on the site of your child care, though it's not right on the homepage. Even your main images are searchable, however, and it's a good practice to add several pieces of information to each image, especially when you consider that most other churches are not indexing their online photos properly.

(image) Bluemound Asset Management uses a single, non-rotating main image with animated images below (not seen in photo).

(image) Organichic uses two main images that rotate. You could have ten if you want.

Main Article

Importance 7/10

Difficulty 2/10

This is the Welcome article. Or sentence. Written words that tell people where they are. The only challenging part might be to keep it to a paragraph, but it should be short and to the point. You are trying to get people to check out your more in-depth articles on other pages, not learn everything there is to know on the main page. But you have to say something, even if it's a simple welcome to our website message or your mission statement.

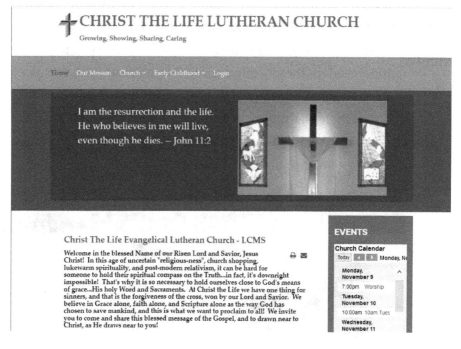

(image) This main article is about the right length.

Sidebar

Importance 5/10

Difficulty 6/10

While websites used to be designed with a menu on top and on the side, the sidebar has become more of a location for ads and links to other content, like popular or newest articles. You could add a news feed from your synod, too. However, a sidebar isn't really required to make the page look the perfect width, and it gets bounced further down the page when in mobile mode, so some sites do away with the extra information on the sides, especially since it requires extra work over simply adding content to the site. Most of the sites I design do use a sidebar because it feels natural as a designer to have something next to an article. It's a good way to remind readers there's other content to be read. You can also use a module in the sidebar as a place for important announcements, though an announcement "module" could be put almost anywhere on a webpage. Try to avoid pop-ups, unless you want to annoy site users.

(image) Using a sidebar effectively to display Google events calendar and mp3 player.

Footer

Importance 7/10

Difficulty 4/10

The footer is more important than in the past only because most businesses are adding contact information here, and I read that one of the main issues people have with poor website design is that location is not easy to find. It kind of makes sense to just have it in the footer of each page. The copyright information is not as important. In fact, I can usually tell when a website was designed by the static copyright date (that's not a difficult fix, either). Use this code and then ask your web designer why it was not used before: "Copyright <script> document.write(new Date().getFullYear()) </script> YOURSITENAME". If you really want another menu, it works in the footer, too, as well as links to privacy policies or sitemaps. If nothing else, have your address in the footer.

(image) An example of a footer.

Editing

Importance 9/10

Difficulty 2/10

As a former English teacher, this one disappoints me. Especially on mostly static pages, read the content before and after it's been published, and then remind other staff members that it's fine to make simple edits if they see errors. Your words do not have to appear as if they've been written by Charles Dickens, but your main page content should be free of obvious errors.

Other articles can have some mistakes, but developing a method for staff or volunteers to help edit is probably a good idea, even if it's just a suggestion box of some sort. It's kind of like if you have a pastor who mispronounces a certain last name or the word "Hmong" every week in prayer for a year, you'd want for there to be a way to let him know he's making a mistake without having to do it in front of everyone. A webmaster email works if it's monitored, but some organization of suggestions would be advisable.

Other Pages and Add-Ons

Using Your Website - Content is King

Before I get into all the potential pages for a website and some of the possible add-ons, let's take a moment to discuss content. If I had a way to do it, I would force employees to add content daily before they're allowed to login and do anything else. Maybe weekly, but the point is that a website, like a church, can be vibrant and alive, or it can be stagnant and boring. How many times would you keep going back to a news site if its last news article was from a year ago? You might return to a website on history. Your church has a history, but you need to see it as news so that others see it that way. If your main attraction is a photo album of the 100th anniversary celebration from five years ago, that's just not much of an attraction beyond a few visits.

Content is the main key to having a fresh website. Yes, you can have a dozen pages (categories) on a site, but if you just leave the content there that was there when someone built the site for you, Google will think nothing is happening. And Facebook posts or Google Calendar posts don't show up on your domain as content. We're talking about articles that might discuss theology or the latest fundraiser. Updates of any kind. Each staff member should be responsible for one update a week, maybe more. That's when you will see the true benefits of a CMS. You can't blame your last web designer for that one, unless the task was left out of your hands. LutherNet sites put the task squarely in your hands. I can advise, but only you can write about what's going on with your ministries. Only you can let others know about the grace of God and how it affects those who attend your church. Only you can publish content that promotes your Christ-centered school.

 A CMS editor (WYSIWYG) is a tool that you could compare to using Google Docs or Microsoft Word. That means you can add html, images, video, tables, and you have a lot of formatting options. However, it's not recommended that you change the font for every article or display 10mb photos in all of your articles. You don't want your articles to drive people away in confusion or frustration.

What you want your articles to do is bring people to your site. The more original content you have about a specific topic, the higher you will generally rank. You can hire an SEO specialist to manipulate the words you use a bit, but a lot of it comes down to having the content in the first place. Keep writing. If you create a monthly newsletter, it should be online. That's a copy and paste job. Most of your content can be copied from other content you create. Letters to members or school parents. All of it. Or, you can write a one-paragraph note about something that's coming up or something that's happened. It all counts, it's easy, and it will make your website easier to find.

Static Content or Blogs?

I've seen many folks jump into the Content Management realm thinking everything needed to be blog articles for it to work, which means some categories that will forever have two oddly-formatted articles and seem unfinished. The fact is that most probably half of your CMS website is going to be relatively static, as in a single article that you change once in awhile, rather than a section that has new articles every week.

For example, you might have an About page, a History page, and a Contact page. Those are facts that you can't really add to weekly, and are therefore static pages on the site. It's fine to have these pages because it's expected.

The types of sections that need to be blogs would be ones that focus on news, features about people or events, announcements, photos, videos, etc. I was on a church website recently that hadn't added news for a year, stopped adding sermons, and generally seemed to disappear from updating the site. I wasn't kidding when I wondered whether the church was still open for business, since nothing online indicated anything was going on at the church. While it might be a good way to keep solicitors from bothering to contact you, it's also a good way to keep everyone else from contacting you.

One way to handle a website solo would be to create your static pages and then just have a blog, which would include ALL of the dynamic content (like a Facebook stream). Then you just have to title articles well, like Sermon - 1/5/2015 or News - 4/6/2015. While it's not the recommended way to organize a section, the point is that you need updated content, not websites that confuse those who try to add the content.

My own designs for clients would have a login on the "Frontend" that allows content to be added or edited without having to be in any kind of administrator section of the site. This is something to consider if you have a number of people at varying skill levels trying to help out on the site. In fact, a good CMS will allow user groups, meaning certain people would be allowed to edit certain pages only. Think about how useful that could be if you want the news to be handled by volunteers without having to worry about one of them editing the main page without permission. However, permissions are kind of complicated for a beginner to manage, and it's an added expense on a paid site.

Login

If you're planning on adding to your page, you'll need a way to login and use the CMS. These systems will often have a backend, or administrator page. As a web designer, I mostly use this method of logging in, since I need control over a lot of the page. I have taught some clients to use the administration pages successfully while others prefer to never touch that side of the website. I provide clients with either way of accessing their sites, but keeping users out of the administration panel is probably a good policy for me and for your organization. You simply do not know how quickly a 13 year-old kid or 60 year-old ministry leader can destroy an entire web page until you hand over the keys. You'd be surprised how quickly YOU could do the same.

(image) A front end login page.

Calendar

Importance 10/10

Difficulty 7/10

If you are not using Google Calendar, then try it. I started out using other event calendars on websites I designed, only to realize that was all about me getting it right. When Google gets something right, it's better than my best efforts. You can embed your calendar on any or all pages. http://evanpaydon.com. You can color code different kinds of events. You can even make some events private, like meetings. If your service is the same time each week, make it a recurring event. The embed code from Google works fine on any page, as long as you make the width 100%.

(image) A Google Calendar page.

Contact Information

Importance 10/10

Difficulty 8/10

You should have your address and office phone numbers displayed prominently on all pages, as mentioned in the Footer section. However, you'll want to do the opposite for personal contact information. You should have a form with reCaptcha protection. That's where an actual person needs to type or click in order to send the message. There is one main reason you get Spam: your email address is displayed for web-crawling devices to get the link. It could be at your district page (which you can't control), but it's often on your own website (which you can control).

The best way to combat this spam is to set up a webpage with contact forms. When you get an email from the form, it will have a title like "Inquiry email from yourdomain.org." Those would be the emails to read. Back when I was searching for a church home, I sent out about 20 emails to pastors in the area. I received two replies. Over a decade later, we're still at one of those churches. However, I know from my wife working at the same church that because she gets about 50 pieces of Spam each day, she probably deletes some legitimate emails once in awhile, especially from people not accustomed to trying to get past filters. If you lose the chance at even one new church member a year because of the way your email system is set up, it's a failure, so you need to use a system that works.

If you don't want to create a separate contact page for each church worker, then a general email form that gets distributed based on content can work, too. All of your mail would go to one protected email account that can then be sent out to those who should get the email, or maybe even accessed by multiple employees. I would recommend a separate form for each employee, but it would cost more to create the pages, and it takes more time when someone leaves for another call.

(image) A contact page, currently without reCaptcha.

Map

Importance 10/10

Difficulty 6/10

I have discovered either no map or a photo of a map on
nearly every site that I've seen that does not meet the mobile-
friendly standards, and that's because five years ago, it was
the way to go. Maybe a link to a map. However, it's easy to
have an embedded map. Google lets you copy the code to
embed, so even if your site is old hand-written html, it can be
done. However, all of the CMS options we've mentioned
would have map add-ons, too. This one is too simple NOT to
do, especially for a church, since people must come to your
church to become a member, and maps are useful to
wedding, baptism, and funeral guests.

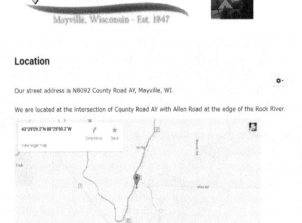

(image) An effective Google Map. Interactive and integrated.

Image Gallery

Importance 7/10

Difficulty 5/10

Even for a CMS, image galleries are complicated. That said, image galleries can be very useful, and you'll want to get images on the site somehow. Let's go through some of the ways you can do this.

Articles

Publishing an image or ten in every article can work. It's time-consuming, and you really need to resize each image. That's why it doesn't work well for those of us looking for a quick way to add content to a website. If you have an image gallery installed on a CMS, you can often have the gallery as part of an article. That works a little better, especially if the gallery resizes for you, but then you miss out on titles and descriptions driving searchers to the website, as you'd want to rename photos to reflect what they are, like sanctuary.jpg.

Gallery Pages

This can be a nice solution if you just want to dump a bunch of related (or unrelated) photos in one place on the site. If you're pressed for time, maybe you can have a folder for each year, and add a dozen representative photos from the year. You could also organize by category and then year, but that requires more time. For example, Church/2015. Of course, if you have all time in the world, the best way would be to have your gallery for each ministry: Church/Altar Guild/2015.

Photos

Pre-2015

(image) A Joomla image gallery – Simple Image Gallery plugin.

Hosted Galleries

Google used to make it difficult to use a hosted gallery, so I recommended Flickr. However, since I found a way to make Google Drive work, this becomes the total best way for you to quickly share huge image galleries. All you need is access to the html editor for an article. (The button that says html or <>). Then, add this code: <iframe src="https://drive.google.com/embeddedfolderview?id=YOURID#grid" width="90%" height="500" frameborder="0"></iframe>

Replace YOURID with the folder name, and be sure the folder is viewable by everyone (hint: the folder name is very long and looks random). Presto! http://luthernet.org/your-new-site/7-colors-photos-and-video

I can still make it work with Flickr or other galleries that allow an embed, but I can't see why that would be necessary, besides the tagging aspect or space (15 GB on Google versus 1 TB on Flickr). Now you can just have a Google account for

ALL of your church photos, organized however you want in folders, with them embedded on your site however you want. When you fill 15 GB, just add another account and keep going. Can you tell I'm excited about this? Granted, it's not a slick image gallery and you will lose out on searches finding the images, but you'll have a better chance of actually adding photos to your site. I'd ALSO get a Flickr account and have it automatically backup your images. If you can figure out how to create folders and streams and groups the right way, you can create an image gallery like the one in the photo below.

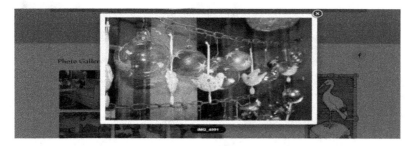

(image) A Flickr gallery on a Joomla page. Great because it does not redirect to Flickr and acts as an actual pop-out image gallery.

(image) A Google Drive folder being used as an image gallery of sorts.

Document Sharing

Importance 8/10

Difficulty 4/10

If your mind is working right now, you can see the usefulness of Google Drive embedding as a DOCUMENT sharing tool. The main thing to remember in Google Drive is to share folders, not files. Make a Shared Document Folder for everyone, add files you want church members to use into that folder, share it to the website, and done. Updated child care form? Delete the old one and add a new one. You can allow those members you trust to EDIT, but it's viewable by everyone. All a parent would have to do is print a copy to edit and bring it in, or download it as a Word version.

I have to admit that there are other options to do this on the site, but I can't see how anyone would bother if Google Drive allows the embedding of its folders. One Drive also allows embedded folders (get the code right in One Drive), but it seems to provide just a link to the folder, not a true grid view. Using either is better than uploading to websites, in general.

If you still want uploaded documents, it can be done on your CMS, but I will be advising against it in my future jobs, unless a client is looking to sell those documents.

one less day

Embedded One Drive Folder, not as a grid.

Public

Letters of Recommendation:

Carroll University   University of Wiscon   Wauwatosa West   Letters of Recomme

References:

(images) Google Drive folders and One Drive folders can be embedded on your website. http://luthernet.org/portfolio/lisa

Videos

Importance 5/10

Difficulty 5/10

Video should be hosted on YouTube or another remote site. You can embed the video easily in articles using a simple component that is either built into a CMS or available for free. People will not generally find your YouTube channel before your website, so the point is to have the content on your actual site. Same thing goes for social media. Go ahead and start a Facebook page or a Twitter account, but don't expect potential members to be impressed by scrolling through to find useful information. Those accounts should be set up to interact and drive them to your website, which is like the rock on which your online presence is built.

There are plenty of wrong ways to deal with videos, and there are plenty of ways to make it nearly impossible to handle for a church staff. Here's a scenario that might be of interest: our church was recording DVDs using an old-fashioned linear editing device, meaning the crew had to hit a record button on a giant console. The camera was DVD-quality. Therefore, we made DVDs in DVD-quality.

We wanted to upgrade, so we got a really high-end camera. At 30 frames per second, it would be about 2 GB for 10 minutes. We had it set to 24 fps, like in a movie, which looks cool as a movie, but this was for people to watch baptisms and weddings. The problem is that we couldn't just dump the whole service on YouTube because of worries about song copyright, so we had to edit the file. If you've ever tried to edit a full HD video on an underpowered laptop, you know it's a chore. Basically, a lot of crashing and gnashing. We tried converting to lower res video to edit. But that takes a long time per video, too.

While YouTube's new service of taking copyrighted music out of videos (Beta) might be the eventual solution, the camera even makes that difficult because it separates out each 10-15 minute chunk at around 2 GB, meaning you'd still have to edit and render a single video to put on YouTube.

The best solution depends on your needs. Our church wants to use the camera at its full awesomeness, which means 500GB of storage a year just to store services. Since external hard drives die every five years or less, it starts to get pricey. If you like cinematic, then 24 fps might be good. TV is generally 30fps, though. Unless your pastor does a lot of fast movements, you probably don't need 60 fps.

We might be sticking with 1080 lines of resolution, but the old way of burning a DVD was around 500 lines. 720 would likely be a decent compromise for churches looking to keep file sizes smaller. Of course, some cameras will allow 720p or 1080i (progressive or interlaced). Again, you have to weigh quality against size. If you're planning on recording and selling baptism and wedding videos, use 1080 at 24fps for that cinematic feel. If you just want to record the service for shut-ins, use 720 at 30fps and burn it to a DVD, and then ask yourself why you bought the camera in the first place. If you really don't care, edit the video and then save it for email (240 lines of blurriness). Now you can put the video on a CD and really wonder why you bought the camera.

Best advice: **get as much of the video as you can onto YouTube as quickly as you can.** Save originals if you need to, but YouTube allows you to download mp4s of the video. If you only want to put the sermon online, consider just recording the sermon. A decent microphone is less than $100. A decent camera with an input for a microphone is less than $500. Take the card out, upload, delete, and set for next week. If you have that amazing camera, use it for making your own show or for wedding memories to be edited by a pro.

Once the video is on YouTube, be sure to fill out descriptions and add tags. You can fit about 20 tags on each video, and the more the merrier, from what I understand. Don't underestimate the power of YouTube to bring new folks to your church. I've seen videos pop up on the top ten of Google well before a website. If all those other Calvary churches do not have videos, you will be ranked higher, and if the four other similar churches in town have not added any videos, then yours will be seen. It's that simple.

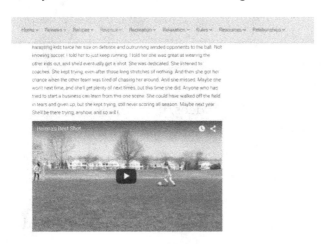

(image) Video embedded in an article.

Website Content, AGAIN

Importance 10/10

Difficulty 3/10

Sure, I discussed it once, but I think it's important to reiterate that content needs to be updated at least weekly. However, your embedded videos and documents count as that content if you create a new article each time you add one to the site. So, videos should be created in a blog fashion. So should image galleries or links to Google Folders with images. For example, create an article entitled VBS 2015. Embed a video and an image folder, and write that it was fun in the article text. One sentence and a lot of imagery. If you have the YouTube account and the Google Drive account, the whole process from start to finish is less than 10 minutes, and your site will look fresh and new to viewers and Google. Even better if you do add a full description in the article text.

Community Pages

Importance 5/10

Difficulty 10/10

Assuming you have all the right content in all the right places, a community-type system on your site could be the greatest answer to a question you probably have yet to ask. Most churches will do this using Facebook, but a CMS like Joomla can do it on the site, with obvious advantages. Creating a closed community site within your CMS allows you to have profiles for every church member, forums, blogs, and articles, as well as information only viewable by administrators. When I set one of these up for my church, I did it as a ministry-only system, meaning each ministry had its own profile with information about the ministry, fully searchable by spiritual gifts desired. I told others it was the greatest ministry website ever created, and it was, but it was only partially realized as a meaningful tool, mostly because the church wasn't sure it wanted all members to participate, making it less useful.

http://immanuelbrookfield.org/serve/index.php?option=com_comprofiler&task=usersList&Itemid=88 - this site may be down now, and I was unable to gain access to the database to recreate it elsewhere. However, you can get the general idea here: http://cureforthepain.com/spiritual-pain/archived-articles/community

While a community website like this one takes months of development, it could be the tool your church needs to stay ahead of the competition, especially when you consider the amount of interaction possible.

(image) Using Community Builder for Joomla to create a ministry page with over 100 listed.

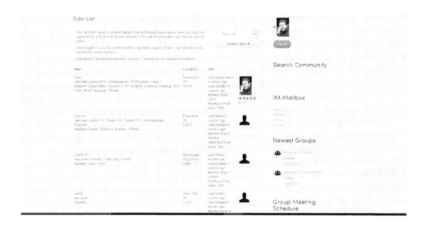

(image) Using Community Builder to create a list of tutors on Educabana.com. This is a closed group, with it only being searchable by members of the website.

Email Newsletters

Importance 10/10

Difficulty 7/10

You'll want to send out newsletters to your church members. You can use a paid system or you can set one up yourself on a CMS. I've set up systems that have no monthly charges, though they may not be as powerful as some of the paid options out there. The point is to get the emails out to church members. I would not mess with installing a component yourself unless you're confident in using a CMS, but it can save you some money, since Constant Contact costs $20 a month for up to 500 email addresses (November 2015). This is not a terrible price, but it does increase to $35 for 501 or more. If you're doing it all yourself and using a shared hosting plan, you'll have to throttle your emails, meaning not sending out more than a certain number an hour. (Shared hosting plans have to do this to try to limit Spam from being sent out.) With paid newsletter services, you don't have to worry about volume, just payments: 600 church members = $35 a month or $420 a year.

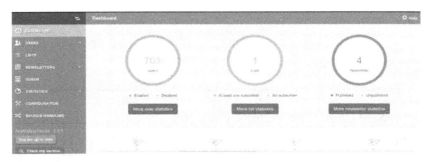

(image) Using a FREE email newsletter tool (Acymailing) on Joomla to send newsletters.

Reader Interaction

Importance 2/10

Difficulty 7/10

You can have like and share buttons, comments, or ratings for some or all of your articles. However, I have not seen this add-on used on very many church websites, and you probably don't want comments on some of your articles. The problem with WordPress (for some) is that comments are turned on by default for all articles. You'll want to change this because of the amount of garbage you'll have to sift through in order to find one legitimate comment. I use comments and like buttons on my writing websites, but that's probably a different case than church articles. I know Joomla still has an "Email" button built into articles, so people will be able to send the links to friends and family that way. Honestly, photo and video pages might benefit from being able to share on Facebook, so just consider the pros and cons, and then ask for the add-on if you want it. http://satisfamily.com has a system that allows likes and comments.

(image) Comments and social media interaction in use on a website.

Embedded Content

Importance 3/10

Difficulty 6/10

You can embed news feeds from your synod (http://luthernet.org/your-new-site) or maybe an online gradebook. Sometimes it works well. When I designed a church site for my wife, I added a Bible Quote of the Day embed. I've also used interesting articles from The Free Dictionary (https://sites.google.com/site/brianjaegerenglish/teachers/home) on my educational sites. Embedded content can make your site more attractive or usable to those who show up, but it will not help you in the search engines, so don't think having it is a replacement for writing. Don't forget the Google Calendar.

Another type of embedded content would be Google Ads. I hate them as much as the next guy, but Google rewards websites that get a lot of traffic, the ads are catered to what the user has been searching for, and it's extra income, maybe even enough to offset hosting fees (I charge $10 a month). If nothing else, if you create a separate Donations page, throw an ad on it and suggest people click on it (about $.25 a click; more if they buy anything).

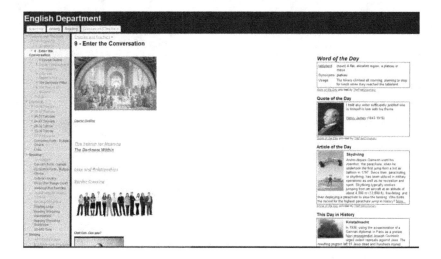

(image) Embedded content on the right side of a Google Sites page.

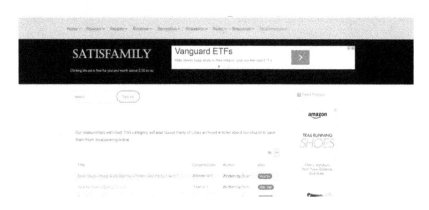

(image) Embedded ads.

CMS Updates

Importance 10/10

Difficulty 9/10

CMS updates come in two flavors: minor and major. Minor updates can often be done with one click of a button. Major updates often warrant looking into a new site. If your CMS is newer, it can probably handle the minor updates for some time, as developers of the systems have realized the importance of maintaining users by avoiding difficult upgrades. If your CMS is hosted by one of the big online hosts that promises automated upgrades, that's great, until web technology passes the company by and they avoid those upgrades because it would be too difficult. This does happen, and a company would often rather lose a few sites a year than try to fix the problems. An open source CMS goes the other way, often creating several updates a year that give developers headaches, especially if add-ons stop working properly.

Ask anyone you're thinking about using as a web developer about the update policy. You should really expect to pay something every two years or so in order to keep the site up to date. My company just does it for free, but that has meant a lot of missed opportunities for added income, and big companies don't like missed income. I've learned to avoid add-ons that are just fun rather than necessary because those are the first to create problems during an update. Because of that, I can do even a major Joomla update (that costs $500 minimum) for free to those who pay for my services. However, if I was hosting 100 sites, I would not be able to do it so efficiently, which is why companies want to charge or conveniently forget about your site after a couple of years. Just remember that, no matter what, you OWN the content you've created for the site. Don't start over with that part of the site. The rest can be recreated.

Major Design Changes

Importance 6/10

Difficulty 8/10

If your site is starting to look a little old compared to the competition, even if it's mobile-friendly and runs fast, you might want a major design change. This is not always such a big deal. I just did one for a client that took less than three hours. The site went from 2010 to 2015 with a template change and an updated framework, all still in the same Joomla CMS. A few items disappeared from the positions because of the upgraded framework, but the process is not difficult for someone who knows where to look. If that's not you, updating a template or theme in a CMS might be better left to a pro, but you can certainly change the templates all you want in the online website builders. You might want to time yourself, however, since making a design look good and work well can take a lot more time and effort than you might think.

If you have a CMS and a major or minor design change in mind, you might want to ask around before you go and drop a website completely. While the original designer might refuse to make changes (or not even know how), someone in your congregation might be well-versed in at least adding a new header image or changing out a template in WordPress. If the volunteer destroys a site you were going to replace, then you just replace it, but you could save thousands just by making a couple of phone calls. Case in point, my church wanted some changes to a WordPress site. I know of several church members who have used WordPress. Even though I am not a WordPress pro, I could probably add a new theme and change a few menu items. Instead, they bought a new site. The costs for the new site were not expensive, but you also have to look at what you SPENT on the old site (which wasn't even broken).

Categories

In this section, I'll talk about some common categories for church websites. This is not an all-inclusive list, and your church might need a dozen more or half of the ones mentioned. However, I'll try to argue for the importance of certain content or add-on categories that will give you an idea where to start, as well as what kind of page it should probably be.

Static Content Pages

These pages do not change much, if ever.

History

You can have the whole handout you provided at the anniversary celebration if you want. Have a group or class make an interactive timeline to embed: http://wildwestallis.com/ using http://www.dipity.com/ . Fun! And that's not always true of church history pages.

Location

Have photos of the church, school, and child care here. And a map. It's also a good place for a welcome video tour. If all you have is the address, that can be done in the footer. This page would be a good candidate for an image gallery, even if you want to use the simpler Google Drive format listed earlier to house most photos.

Staff

List your staff (with photos). You can also have this done as contact forms, but it's not totally necessary. Just give a brief synopsis of who they are and what they do. Embedding a

Linkedin profile might look professional, too. I know from having a wife working at church that people do not always understand who is specifically in charge of what. A staff page is a perfect place to have a list of duties.
http://luthernet.org/our-team

Giving

You can easily embed a Donate button using PayPal, but you could also have a document that shows yearly donations. The same kind of information you might distribute to the congregation could be on a page like this, but it should also contain specifics about what was done with the money. Maybe thank yous for major contributions or how to go about leaving one. Don't overestimate the knowledge members (or non-members) have about the good the money does in a church. This page would also tie in with any fundraising pages. I've done a 3% Amazon fundraising add-on that you use, but you can do the same thing yourself as a church by signing up as an affiliate...you'd get 4% commissions. Since I didn't make very much money on small commissions, I abandoned making it a big part of my business, but any church can give it a shot, or contact me for how I can set a 3% system up for you. brian@passiveninja.com. I also mentioned Google Adsense previously. If you have a Giving page, then a Google ad is not more cold than a PayPal Donate button, and if you explain the reasons and the good, people should give you a few clicks.

Church / School / Child Care

Many churches will have categories for their main activities that are subdivided further. Since many churches also run schools and child care facilities, it makes sense to divide them. You just have to be careful when it comes to photos and other potentially shared categories. An example might be Staff: do you want one staff page, or do you want one staff page for each of your three main categories?

Ministries

Many churches make this a static content item, but if you have 100 ministries, each one could be its own article. See the Community Pages section for more on how you could create something special with your ministries pages. If nothing else, list them somewhere.

About

The About or About Us page is pretty self-explanatory, but it should be a bit more than the welcome message. You could have a statement of beliefs as part of it or as a subcategory. Like the other static content, craft it well once and focus on the blog-type sections.

Dynamic Content Pages

These categories are best set up as blogs with weekly or daily updates. At least monthly.

News

I've seen church websites with five different news-like categories and others with one. If you have a plan that includes monthly updating in different categories, go ahead and create all the news pages for organizational purposes. The problem is when one category gets updated and the other sits empty. One method that might work would be to have one category blog per staff member: you'd share responsibility and accountability.

Some examples of news categories I've seen include News, Articles, Newsletters, Blog, Q and A, Pastor's Thoughts, Updates, and plenty more.

Media

You can have Photos or Videos pages under any other category or under a Media heading. I've discussed the importance before, and you will want to update these just as often as your News categories. People like seeing photos of events at church. Google Drive and YouTube make this easier than you might think. Many churches will have a separate Sermons category.

Other Ideas

When I worked on some redesign ideas for our church, I wanted to have the "I Want to…" category with such items as Get Married or Find a School. The church ended up choosing an "I'm New" category--similar. I have also seen a Testimonials page on church websites, and you should consider this, either as written messages from current members or as videos. Call it Members if you want. Some churches will have Resources as another category that might include articles or just links to resources that work for Bible study or enrichment. I've seen Prayer pages, too. Mainly, I would say that if you can get staff members and volunteers to be passionate about a certain category, go ahead and create it for the site. If you just think it's a good idea, nobody is going to update the content enough for it to work, so wait until someone else thinks it's a good idea.

Keep it Going – More Content Ideas

Daily Updates

Your new website is only as good as its content, and your content is only as good as how often you write it. Each article does not have to be a work of art, but it will take some work. You need to be willing to put that time in or else the money for redesigning your site will have been wasted.

Relevant, Researched Topics

The topics for your content should include current events, current people (like new members), and current multimedia (like photos or sermons).

One Person of a Team

A team of people working on the site seems to make the most efficient way of keeping the site current. However, teams tend to wait for someone else to take the lead, especially if it's a team of volunteers. I'd say give the team a try at first. Ask for volunteers and ask for a weekly commitment from each. When that doesn't work, then you can force someone who works there already to deal with it, or you could pay someone else. Hopefully, you will get a team of volunteers who love mundane activities, a list does not normally include pastors, teachers, or others who actually work at your organization.

Make it "Evergreen," Even With Borrowed Content

I've been writing content for online publishing for a long time, but I'd never really considered whether or not the content I wrote was evergreen, or something that would last for years as a relevant online piece. For example, this article could have been written five years ago and it will be fairly relevant several years into the future. Therefore, I won't have to update it much for it to continue to be read. Ministry descriptions, biographies, histories, and many other pages work. Just be sure to pay attention to when someone quits or passes away. If you must borrow content, do it. I'm not talking about stealing. The Free Library is nice because it updates daily and looks professional, but you can find other free content out there, too. You can repost Wikipedia content if you add a link, so you don't necessarily have to hire research assistants to get some content on the site.

Link Away

It used to be that external links were very important in determining the ranking of a site. While this may not hold true the same as it once did, relevant links are still very important. The idea is that you try to get a site with more traffic to link to you if you promise the same in return. For example, if you can get the local library or your church's synod to link to you, you benefit because more people may use those sites or at least have the perception that the governing bodies endorse you.

Data

Important, But Not End-All

What's your data-driven goal? The world as a whole is too hung up on data. It can be useful, depending on your goal, but churches and schools have bigger missions than bowing down to the data aggregators. For example, I'd bet polling data would indicate that the pastor at your church should give shorter sermons. Does that make it the right thing to do? Is it so important that traffic increase to your website by 20% every month? Is that even possible? Do you give up and say Satan won if you fail? You probably want to create metrics to measure if the site is effective. I can't stop you from doing that. However, you might realize that people expect sites exist but don't necessarily make decisions about churches or schools solely based on those websites. While you can maybe drive someone away with a pastor's wife Facebook page, most other incarnations of a web presence are pretty standard.

Match Similar Sites in Your Area

If you really want to get into the numbers, I recommend you just try to match the similars. Find churches or school with similar attendance and then look up their online rank compared to yours. There are some services that will give Alexa ranks or similar scores. Look around for a free tool that seems to give usable results. Then make it your goal to match the top competitor in the area. Make sure you check out the comparable sites, too. Maybe they all pale in comparison to your new CMS, but maybe a few have items you could use. For example, every car I've ever owned has had one or two features that seem ingenious, and only found on that car. What if someone took all those cool and unique features and put them on one car? Make that your website.

Unique Visitors and New Visitors

As you are working to get more people to visit your site, pay attention to unique views and new, relevant visitors. Is a hacker looking for a backdoor to your site from Russia an important visitor? Is your own IP address important? You're looking for people coming from referring pages like those with whom you've exchanged links or from Youtube or Facebook. You're looking for unique search terms that you've somehow captured. For example, before our church got redesigned by a persuasive yet skilless businesswoman, I checked it's top ranking search terms because she said her company would fix all the problems with the site. Our site was in the top 10 on Google for something like why god or why jesus, and you can imagine that such an obvious search phrase would be awesome to have. However, today the site is a CMS that has been abandoned and the search term longer even registers on Google after I add the church name because that specific static content that had been there for years as a beacon to anyone asking the same question was now gone. Find out what people might be looking for an give them what they need.

Stat Access

My host gives me access to tools that are simple and provide some data. This is in the Cpanel. Google Analytics is more robust and provides a lot more data. I do not enjoy using it, and I'm not sure any of my clients would really understand it, but it's not a bad idea to have an account and add your code to the webpage in order to look at it once in a while. More than likely, someone at church loves Google Analytics and can help you see the light. I do like using Google Webmaster Tools. It does not provide the data needed to make big decisions, but it does allow me to index pages and add sitemaps in order to help Google see the hard work I put into my websites. If nothing else, be sure you have some arrangement for seeing some kind of stats related to your website.

That's not really all there is to know, but it's a good start. You can stop here and get to work or you can keep reading, especially if you're still convinced you've got it all figured out. Since the internet and website design keeps changing, none of us will ever have all of it figured out, and that's something to remember when the salesmen come knocking at the door. You should know some of right questions to ask at this point, at least.

More Articles and Resources

Here are some other articles I've written that are related to church website design.

Ten Ways Your Web Guy is Overcharging

I am a web designer, and maybe I should not be revealing how others in my field can overcharge, kind of like the secrecy kept by magicians. The problem in that there are all kinds of companies that try to reveal the truth behind the magic by offering cheap websites and hosting, but those companies aren't doing you any real favors. The purpose of this article is to show you that finding an honest and reliable web guy is just as important as an honest mechanic or reliable yard work guy, but all of us will overcharge if given the chance. This is just to give you some idea how and why it happens with web designers.

1. Charging Hours Instead by the Job
A web guy should be charging by the job because you would never pay if you knew how many hours it takes (SOMETIMES). Here's the deal: it can often take me less than 8 hours to fully set up a $500 website. OR it could take me 8 hours to almost set it up and then three hours to figure out why one component is generating an error. OR it could take 8 + 3 + another 6 hours figuring out that the new host requires a php.ini file in every folder instead of just one, which is causing all of the problems in the first place.

Most clients are perfectly happy when a job is done, and it's always a job they could not have figured out for themselves, but that's where the fuzzy honesty can creep in. I recently charged $450 for two Joomla 2.5 to Joomla 3.4 upgrades that included adding a newsletter component and a form for collecting user information. I made about $75 an hour on that job, until you factor in the 5+ hours and frustration I spent trying to fix a header issue caused by the upgrade. Those were also five hours I could not have added to the bill, since it would have appeared I didn't know what I was doing, so the other parts of the bill had to cost a little more. Not a big deal, since I priced the job out via comps online at over $1000, but still something to consider. Would you really pay someone $100 an hour to learn how to fix the site he broke in updating it? No, but you might pay a total of $1000 for a job that included it as part of the process. If your web guy knows it all, all the time, try to pay by the hour (even though he'll want to charge an hour for 35 minutes, a soda, and an online game. The main lesson is that if you're happy with the service for the price, don't worry too much, but the truth is that I could charge you three hours to make a change that takes me ten minutes. And if you question it, I could always say there was an administrator issue with a trouble tracker that was totally out of my hands. Basically, a web guy COULD pull the same stuff your in-house IT guys could also do all the time.

2. Consultation charges

I just saw a competitor offer an hour free up front and then change $90 an hour once you're a customer. That's probably not that bad of a rate, as long as you're not talking to his unpaid intern for either or both consultations. Expect to pay $50 to $100 for web guy consultations. I give way too many away free over email with "friends" (clients). The main issue here is that a five minute Google search might help more than the $100 consultation, or it might at least cut the consultation time in half. That's all your web guy is going to do, anyhow. Search the internet and then apply fixes, AFTER the $100 consulting fee.

I encourage website owners to take ownership and try a few things. Yes, they will need me, but they will often solve minor issues without a phone call. But that is why I have to set a cost of interaction, since some people will try to abuse it. Conversely, your web guy might charge $100 for 45 minutes while he's driving in to work and another hour for a 15 minute email once he gets there.

3. Site Updates and SEO

A lot of the CMS stuff I use allows me to set it to do automatic updates. If you are being charged $50 a month for this kind of maintenance, it's probably way too much. Yes, there are services needed, but routine maintenance is just that, and often hands-off. I added search engine optimization to this category because people charge just as much for just as little return. Google has tried to figure a way around cheating for placement for years. SEO folks will still sell you on their services, but the better idea is to CREATE GOOD CONTENT. You don't need constant minor site updates or optimization of poorly-written words. Just write something relevant, like this article, and it will matter to Google and your customers.

4. Site Upgrades

This is also known as rebuilding the website. Theoretically, it's easier in a CMS like Joomla or WordPress, but these can be a total pain. Plus, your original designer almost never lets you in on the secret that his design will be mostly obsolete in three years, and nearly impossible to upgrade if you wait another two years. Really, it's not fair to the designer to expect free upgrades, but it's not fair to the consumer to never tell them there will be major updates at some point. It would be like selling a car and the customer assuming the brakes, suspension, transmission, and engine are all made to run forever, as long as there's oil and gas inside. I just looked into a Joomla 1.5 to 3.4 upgrade, and I don't really want to bother. Joomla 1.0 to 3.x is impossible. I've even had more issues than I want to remember updating 2.5 to 3.4. There are so many variables that your web consultant will want to charge enough to cover all bases, so I've seen these kind run $300 to $1500. You might be better off starting over, and that sucks when using a CMS with the main purpose being to manage content.

5. Component Add-ons

The first few sites I built, I added these things like crazy. Then one component failed. Then another couldn't survive a minor upgrade. Then there are the updates to the extensions: more time. Now I try to add about $100 per add-on. Some companies might charge $500 or $1000. They do it based on time they know they will need to keep it running. Like I told a client recently, "The fewer moving parts we can use for the same result, the better." In this way, building a website is like the poetry I write, in that I try to create the most emotion with the fewest words possible. Web design companies deserve to get some money for adding these components, but I've seen $10 monthly upcharges on hosting for adding a YouTube embedder. If your web guy can explain the extra cost, fine. If not, the component took five minutes to install and twenty seconds once a year to update, and it was free, so just keep that in mind if your hosting costs a lot more than what we can do at Passive Ninja.

6. Hosting Packages

If you're not getting a dedicated host, your hosting is probably worth about $10 a month when buying through a web guy. Decide with what is being offered and if you need the add-ons. Most of those add-ons exist already in the C-Panel, but you're just paying to have access to them. Do you need a new email address or analytics? Do you need a $100 e-commerce solution when you can sell stuff securely using PayPal and my $15 a month option? The way I do it is to look at my own cost and time/cost and then double the cost. The prices I have seen from other companies indicate they have a lot more costs, but that makes sense, located in the trendy side of town, employing twenty heads at $100,000+ each. I'd be charging a lot more for hosting, too, but the real truth is that they get the same Cpanel and 99% uptime as me. Sure, they have five socially-awkward guys ready to fix your problem before noon each day, but those problems don't tend to exist, anyhow.

7. Opt-in Sites

My sister was all excited about opt-in marketing. She'd learned it was the thing to do. I wasn't sure what she meant, but I had just set up a site for another client that allowed him to collect email addresses and send emails out to over a thousand potential clients because of a form and newsletter component I added to the page. His business has doubled in the last year, partially because of this type of marketing. A lot of companies will charge you a lot of money to house, store, and send emails for you. Like I said, my sister asked for it, and I added it to her site for about $300. I also added a "free book" offer. Pretty sweet: free book put in shopping cart, which is really a form to join the site and get a newsletter. Newsletter promotes other paid-items to people who wanted the initial book. The best part about me or another honest freelancer setting this up for you is that once you have it, it's yours. AcyMailing is totally free. J2Store cost me $30 (and I pass a small portion to clients). Community Builder is free unless you want to add subscriptions.

8. Shopping Carts or Subscription Sites

There are plenty of free or cheap solutions for your web guy to implement. I use J2Cart for shopping carts and CB Subs for subscription websites. Think of ways you can sell an item or a service, especially a recurring service. Passive Ninja is a specialist in creating websites that generate constant money, but you have to be the specialist in generating customers. One of my clients told me that the CRM components used for insurance sales costs so much that he wouldn't make enough each month to cover the costs. A web designer can't operate very long with that type of mindset. Once I set it up, there are no extra fees beyond the normal hosting. You sell, you get rich. Simple.

9. Site Ownership
Some web guys want to try to maintain control over what goes on. Too much control. As long as I warn a client (and get paid for fixing it), I am fine with the client trying to do as much as possible to the site. It's yours. If you need me to replace a photo or add a new article, you need to use Blogger instead of a nice CMS. Web designers build this kind of ownership in so that they can continue to nickel and dime you forever, as they allow the site itself to get older without needed updates. Even the big companies have poor reputations for this sort of behavior.

10. Outsourcing
Did you know that I could potentially get a contract from you and outsource the whole thing to India? I get an email a day with requests to outsource my web jobs to them, which means I could sign you up, get $1000 for a site, play golf all day, and then check the work from New Delhi after dinner. I'm sure this is not a trend for freelancers or even fancy downtown web design boutiques, but someone is using these folks. Technically, I can't compete with what they can accomplish, time-wise. Even if I'm fast, like 8 hours for a pretty darn good site, and it takes them 16 hours, I could still make $900 for hiring out and playing golf. Small spelling errors and lackluster images aside, they will charge about $5 an hour to do the work. If you find out that any aspect of your website is outsourced, including your trouble tickets, your web guy is ripping you off. The problem is that your web guy even has to deal with hosting plans that are completely outsourced and trouble tickets that hang in purgatory for months. However, at least try to keep most of the job local, which keeps excuses local and control local.

Newer is not Always Better in Web Design and Technology

A friend and I were discussing some purchases made by a non-profit we both hold dear to us, and I was lamenting the waste of money that had gone into technology. I made a statement that I'd probably heard before, but you probably don't hear it very often from someone trying to sell you a new website or technology-based service: newer isn't always better; better is better. Let's look at a few illustrations to prove my point.

We can start with my former employer, a school district. Those in charge of technology spending seemed to spend as if their own jobs depended on it--like if they found simple, free or cheap solutions with teacher input, someone might question *their* value. Actually, I think I hit the nail dead-center. I found free component after free component that did most of what their paid services could do, and most of the licenses they were purchasing were $10,000 a year, but it made them look like they were in charge of this important part of the school district. Basically, they had no incentive to find efficiencies because the money spent made it appear as if they were doing their jobs, whereas I, as an individual teacher, could not afford to spend any money, so I found free solutions.

I know, it doesn't make sense. However, neither does changing everything because something new is available. We changed teacher websites four times in the twelve years I was teaching. In that time, I kept ONE personal teaching page that was better than the school-bought systems when I put it together, and, in a lot of ways, better than the last sites the school district was implementing as I was leaving (Google Sites, except those I built: Teaching site https://sites.google.com/site/brianjaegerteachingpage/

Department Site
https://sites.google.com/site/brianjaegerenglish/). Anyhow,
the point is that the district could obviously figure out when
websites were bad, but it relied on salesmen to outline how
the sites could be good. Do you know what the answer was,
each and every time? Go with our company. That's it. As if
their companies were going to do anything more than look
slightly newer than the last one; as if teachers were suddenly
going to update a new system. Nope. Newer was just newer.
Better would have been getting people to change, not
changing the website again, but salesmen can't sell new
people, so they sell new websites.

Of course, as a new business owner, I should be a salesman.
I'm just not. I'm a pragmatist who built better websites for my
students than most of you have ever had built for you
corporations. No, they weren't super flashy, but the sites I
built were solid and provided the tools students needed to do
well, and then (and this is REALLY important) I made them
use the sites. When I redesigned the English 9 curriculum, it
was so that computers would be required DAILY, and not
just to send each other silly messages or vote on some dumb
classroom voting thing. You see, the kind of website I built
didn't matter as much as the fact that I was forcing its use,
and that's what made my site better than any other English 9
website ever built in Google Sites.

School districts think that if they go with the next e-learning
site, what I was able to accomplish will happen overnight.
Salesmen, again. Do you realize what you get when you first
set up a educational management system? NOTHING. You
add stuff to the site, like I did with my Joomla site and my
Google Sites site. The online learning pages I created took
hundreds of hours to create. Sure, it's cool that Moodle or the
like can show students their progress, but all those lessons
have to be created by a teacher who couldn't even update a

one-page, template-based page. The right solution, of course, is to pick one solution that can be expanded and train people not only how to use it but WHY to use it. That's it. Then, repeat yearly until it catches on. If you've gone with something like Joomla or WordPress, keep it updated, and show people why it's important to update. No magic. But magic is what has web developers and marketers driving BMWs.

If You Don't Know, You Better Ask Somebody (Honest)

Sometimes it's that simple. Ask someone for help. Maybe that someone is working for your organization, but it might be someone you hire. However, look for someone internally first. Hey, does anyone here have experience using WordPress? Maybe not. Hey, does anyone have a spouse who knows Joomla or Moodle? If you've had a website for a few years and nobody in your organization had gotten at least a little bit good at using it, then nobody's using it at all. None of the CMS options are that difficult. However, hired or not, find someone. The non-profit mentioned at the start of this article was frustrated with a poorly-designed website in WordPress. I'm better at Joomla myself, but someone associated with the organization (of over 1000) would have been able to help. Or, maybe watch some tutorials on YouTube or download a guide. Instead, (you're not going to believe this) the organization got a new website built in (you guessed it) WordPress. Brand new, as in Hello World, add content here. I'll take a breath and explain for those of you contemplating a mistake like this. Let's say you bought a car. The frame was free, but the design cost something. All you have to do to get a new design is keep the frame and throw another design over it. Maybe fill the tires. Instead, this organization bought a new car on the same free frame. The salesmen were happy to oblige, I'm sure.

Another purchase was that of a video camera. The main purpose of this camera is to show video to older people on DVDs. The old system was a cheapo video camera hooked directly into DVD burner. It was kind of a complicated system, and not everyone was comfortable with it. Instead of training everyone, the solution, as promoted by a likeable salesman, was to buy a several thousand dollar video camera. Those cameras use about 1 GB per minute. I know because I have a DSLR. DVDs hold less than 5 GB. New problem. Also, it records at double the resolution achievable on a DVD. The organization needed better, not newer, and in this case, better would have been learning how to use the DVD burner. Or maybe a cheap $200 video cam like I got my son for Christmas that records in HD with smaller file sizes. But salesmen don't like selling $200 cameras, and those in charge of implementing technology don't like purchasing items that seem simple.

What all of the purchases have in common was me and other people who knew better. I was known as someone who had experience with technology in a way that worked. The problem was that my solutions were often simple and often free or cheap. Plus, I always think about the end-user because my end-users include students, family, and friends. I don't want them to hate me, so I consider how difficult my solution would be for them. The cool part is that when I take it all into consideration, adjust to early comments, and then teach people how to use what I have created, they end up being the best websites anywhere. And it's not because of me as the designer of new sites. It's because I think about what would make a site better while I'm making it newer, because better is better.

Government Money Means More Scrutiny

While it may not be a national trend, some states have opened up ways for students of religious schools (usually Lutheran and Catholic) to use government vouchers to pay for those schools. Parents might also get tax deductions for sending their children to religious schools. While the money and opportunity to educate more students is attractive, churches and schools that accept government money need to be aware of the scrutiny that has not always been part of old system.

Taxpayers will be looking for proof that what you do is beneficial. While these folks might not mind that your classroom is Christ-centered, they will also be looking for more than a religious experience. Most public schools use websites purchased through large corporations that cost the schools upwards of $10,000 a year to run, and many of those school districts have employees on staff who are paid to specifically maintain the web presence. Why? They're trying to sell a product to people who are thinking of spending money elsewhere. Maybe you have a better product, but does your website stack up well against the local public school? Is it even as good as the other local parochial or religious schools?

Parents that transfer over from public schools might be used to lower standards, but public school teachers and administrators have been interacting with parents for years online. Yes, this can be a newsletter, but you should consider class pages for each grade level. Maybe even for each teacher. Get a website using a platform that is expandable, and it has been used successfully in education sites all over the world. Parents might want to know whether Junior has homework, but is Twitter where you want your teachers posting this?

Students at most public schools have to learn how to use teacher websites to get assignments. Not all teachers and not all assignments, but it does happen quite a bit. The best place to find those teachers and their assignments is on the school's homepage, not on some Facebook page set up by the teacher or a classroom parent, and not on some other system the teacher just likes better. Even if you use an inline frame to publish the assignments from another site, YOUR school website needs to be where parents, students, and the outside world goes to see that your school is rigorous and relevant. You can link, embed, or improve upon any system. We've done this before using Joomla and Google Docs to create some of the best teacher websites for students. Don't be afraid to integrate inexpensive solutions to your existing site.

It might not happen right away, but someone will start to question your website and its ability to function properly in a world filled with expensive web solutions at other schools. In fact, you're even competing against online-only schools for the same students. Do you think their websites are lacking? With a website built on a CMS, you can compete with the public schools, the online schools, the fancy parochial schools, and the homeschools because you're website will be better than theirs. And that's before they consider your amazing staff and the fact you can deliver a sustained moral education.

Evangelism is NOT Hiding, Resting, or Pretending

As a lifelong Lutheran, I have the right to make an observation about our evangelical behaviors, and it's not entirely positive. If you are looking for the #1 reason for a decline in the Lutheran Church, it probably has to do with the lack of evangelism, even while many of our churches (and even synods) have the word as part of the title. Ironic, yes, but not useful for recruiting and maintaining membership, A website from LutherNet.org is a good start in being evangelical, but there are a few traps you'll want to avoid as you bolster your online presence.

 Hiding. We have a Lutheran college about three blocks away. We rarely see the students out, even when our family walks around on their campus. The only time I was ever invited to the campus was in order to discuss concerns about students not treating the neighborhood like their own, and my suggestions about having students interact more in the community were ignored.. When I looked the college up on Google, one review said the campus was secretive and elitist. Seemed true from my experience. I grew up in a different neighborhood where many of the kids went to Lutheran or Catholic schools, which is great, but I was told quite often by them (and their parents) that public schools (and those attending them) were bad. The point is not to isolate ourselves as Lutherans in order to avoid others who have less or with whom we will not commune. Rather, as an evangelical congregation, the point is to at least show others around us the importance of our faith. Invite others. Help others. Talk about your faith with others. Or, just set a good example for others, but don't just be good people hidden away in your school or church. That's not evangelical. Using a website to share your views with other people is an efficient way to come out of hiding without having to ring doorbells. You might want to pick up the trash generated by your facility or have a sign that reminds people to respect the neighborhood, too (like my church does). Wear church t-shirts and do something for the community. People will notice you're not hiding.

Resting. Maybe many Lutherans are good with the fact that Martin Luther did a lot to start the whole Protestant movement. The problem is that Martin Luther died nearly 500 years ago. A lot has happened since then, and Lutherans need to work on adapting to the world as much as other denominations. No, we don't have to give in to anything, but using the tools available in a way that promotes our views is imperative. For example, most Lutheran congregations now have screens of some sort that are used during service, send out emails, or use technology in some way to help spread God's Word. However, you should not neglect the way that unchurched people seek out Truth: on the internet. To be evangelical, you must have an online presence that invites others and tells them about your church. If your site is outdated, it's not being found by those who need to find it most. Martin Luther never rested in his mission.

Pretending. Churches will often pretend to be evangelical by doing things for fellow church members. Think about it: if you have a day of service, and people volunteer to help with lawn care for church members (or the church itself) or participate in various other church-related activities that mostly benefit fellow church members, you're pretending. There is certainly a place for helping each other out, and don't stop doing it, but if that's the alternative to true evangelism, then at least get a website to promote it so that others in the community know which church is generous to its members. A website that is updated and has relevant information for those seeking God can be a very useful tool, and it will be augmented by your acts of kindness that can be added to the site via articles and photos. You can lead by example and be evangelical without having to step out of your comfort zone, but you likely can't do it with your current, outdated website, so contact LutherNet today. Besides, those who THINK all of your mission work is internal will get a chance to see the truth, as long as you update the site with articles about what you do.

Keep in mind that Lutheran churches do not attempt to hide, rest, or pretend. It's just a bit easier than the alternative. A website can really help get people involved at church, but it can also help the outside world see the benefits of visiting your church. Whether you are reaching rural America for Christ or otherwise engaging your community (EYC), it's much easier to do when you have a decent website.

Beware: Your Church is a Huge Target

I'm not a salesman, but if I was, I'd target churches, especially if I was looking to make the most amount of money with the least amount of work. The two factors that make churches appealing to those who want to make a quick buck include lack of knowledge and trust. Because of a church's limited staff, a lot of decisions are made by folks who are not trained in making the decisions. Beyond that, the church employees are good, trusting people. Both of these factors make your church a target, and not just for web design services.

Let's begin with web design because that's what we know here at Luthernet. Most of the companies you hire to work on a site will have the following types of employees, some of which might overlap: UX/UI, Designer, Coder, Manager, Graphic Designer, Junior Web Designer, SALESMAN, office assistant, and more. I know some of these jobs often have different titles, and some will have the same person doing three of the jobs. The point is that before the salesman gets to you, the new site you purchase has to support several other $100,000 a year jobs. There's probably a CEO taking a cut, as well. You're supporting a lot of people if you buy a website this way, but you also deal with a huge markup. They are good, and they know they have to hire good salesmen who will tell you there's some need for their services on a website that, in all honesty, does not require most of their most important skills (like creating shopping carts or mobile apps). Your church is a target because you might not know exactly what you need and you know that quality often costs money. Luthernet web design is kind of like going right to a great mechanic to fix up your car rather than buying a new one that you have built from scratch. That's why our websites are so much cheaper. We pay the UX/Coder/Manager/Designers/Programmers to sell us a way to make you a great site (like owning a car frame), and then it's just about the time to put it all together. They build from the ground up. And I've seen this: a company charging a church $10,000 and taking a year to build a site that would have been a three-day, $1000 makeover for us. When I told a friend (web designer) about this fiasco, he said $10,000 wasn't too bad, probably because he saw it as a $15,000 site.

Another reason your church might be a target is because of the nature of gifts (and salesmen know this). Someone leaves the church $5000 for a specific purpose, but your staff can only think of one item to buy, and therefore you start looking for a single $5000 item. There might not be a worse way to shop, especially when the people making the purchases have no experience with the items being bought, like a new intercom system or artwork for the fellowship hall. On top of that, when these gifts are used, the funds are not part of a specific budget, meaning there's little incentive to save any of it. Because good salesmen can get church staff to trust them, that means the church will be strung along for years to come, often selling upgrades and replacements. If you notice that every electronic item is purchased through the same salesman, you might want to check online prices and reviews on some of the items you own.

Let's say your church has $5000 to spend on video equipment. You record sermons and put them online. Do you need a $5000 camera in the balcony to replace the one worth $35? Maybe, if you intend to use it in other places rather than mounting it permanently, if you have a lot of extra space to store huge files, and if the better quality recordings translate to better quality online videos. However, you might be able to continue using the old camera or buy a $100 replacement. In fact, it's often LESS work for your volunteers to keep things simple. The problem is that your favorite salesman only makes $10 on the cheap camera instead of $500 on the super-duper-pro-cam. Plus, that's easier than selling a dozen different kinds of prosumer cameras and accessories. One item and a day off instead of days of research to help find the right item. Make sure you expect a little work out of your salesmen.

Another dilemma you might be having is the need for screens or computers. You have to get different opinions and quotes. But it's not a bad idea to ask people who attend your church what they might do. For example, as a former teacher, I know that only some teachers really use or want to use SmartBoards. Just about everyone wants computers and projectors, but only some really want the full SmartBoard setup, so it wasn't a surprise that every teacher in my department received $5000 SmartBoard setups when many of us would have preferred full HD hdmi-ready projectors at less than half the cost. At church, the question might be whether to get projectors or replace projectors with huge televisions. If your church is small enough or dark enough, have you even tried a "normal" projector rather than the ones designed specifically for churches? Can you borrow a test TV in the size you're thinking about so that you'll know before week one of the new TV whether or not it works. Have you thought of mounting 4 TVs together to make one big screen? Have you asked your members for ideas? Staff? Someone other than your best salesman?

I remember when I worked at a retail store that the manager told me it was cheaper to continuously buy new soap dispensers because they came with new soap instead of buying refills on the dispensers already owned. This meant a lot of holes in the bathroom wall and a lot of extra work. I don't know how much soap we went through at the store, so I can't say this manager was saving our store a ton of money, but he was impressed with himself. It seemed like small potatoes to me, but I guess if you save enough, it adds up.

Sometimes, you can save on the front end by SPENDING a little extra. Let's say a church is remodeling, and it could rewire for future security, knowing it would cost $10,000 extra now or $20,000 to retrofit the system later. It might be nice to save the $10,000. It also might be nice to see if there's a DIY way to add the security system when you do need it. With a decent plan and some volunteers, that $50,000 security system might run $10,000. Or, it might be too complicated, in which case it was still a good idea to think ahead. Should you lease computers or buy them or have staff/students bring their own? Ask a few people, staff, and parents before the salesman. It depends on what you need, not on what your salesman needs.

Ministry Leader Resources - An Annotated List by Lisa Jaeger

This section contains information about books and websites that might be useful to ministry leaders. It was compiled for Immanuel Lutheran but can be used for your leaders, too.

Books

- Are You Committed? - Jay McSwain, 2007.

An excellent book for leaders and pastors about ministry work and the cycle involved to really mobilize members for ministry.

- Creative Leadership Series The Care And Feeding Of Volunteers - Douglas W. Johnson, 1978.

Gives lots of recruiting techniques.

- The Church of Irresistible Influence: Bridge-Building Stories to Help Reach Your Community - Robert Lewis and Rob Wilkins, 2001.

Great stories of building bridges into the community, based on the experiences of an Arkansas church. An inspiring description and story showing how a church can become an irresistible influence on its neighborhood, community, and world by building bridges over troubled waters to a dying culture through showing the love of God in action (from Amazon.com description).

- The Collaboration Challenge: How Nonprofits and Businesses Succeed Through Strategic Alliances - James E. Austin, 2000.

Austin identifies major alliances and examines how they function, looking at the various stages through which they must pass. He explains the role of top leadership and emphasizes the importance of a strategic "fit" between the two partners. Austin suggests different areas within organizations for alignment as well as ways for partners to analyze the value of their collaboration. He then considers ongoing practical management issues and concludes with guidelines for collaborations and questions that must be addressed (from Amazon.com description).

- Doing Church as a Team: The Miracle of Teamwork and How It Transforms Churches - Wayne Cordeiro, 2005.

This book gives insights into how we can structure today's church into teams much like Jesus had his team of disciples. It covers topics such as how to create a church vision, identify and use members' gifts, prevent burnout, etc. Very inspirational and practical.

- Equipping Church, The - Sue Mallory, 2001.

Hands-on guide to how to create a church environment that equips members for service.

- The Externally Focused Church - by Rick Rusaw and Eric Swanson, 2004.

This book focuses on motivating strategies to bring the Good News of the Gospel from our churches into our wider world through Good Works.

- <u>Find Your Fit - Dare to Act on God's Design for You</u> - by Jane Kise and Kevin Johnson, 1998.

A helpful, PLACE-type resource for teens.

- <u>Growing Dynamic Teams</u> - Group Training Series

A workshop to help your ministry leaders develop effective teams. Even if you have never led a workshop before, you can successfully guide your leaders through this team building experience.

Includes:

Tips on being a great workshop facilitator

Easy preparation, including a checklist of all the steps to lead

A facilitator's guide, including a script to lead you through each minute of this half-day workshop

Reproducible printed handouts for the participants

Reproducible printed copies of the presentation visuals

A CD-ROM with files containing the handouts and presentation visuals

Go to the Group Publishing site - http://store.grouppublishing.com to order (and for more resources too!)

- Leading the Team-Based Church: How Pastors and Church Staffs Can Grow Together into a Powerful Fellowship of Leaders A Leadership Network Publication - George Cladis, 1999.

Great strategies for revitalizing the church structure to be more team-oriented and focused on outreach.

- Participant's Guide Living Beyond Myself Discover Joy Through Serving Others - by Bill Hybels, 1996.

A Biblical examination of servanthood - part of a campaign to have whole churches examine this topic.

- Living a Life on Loan: Finding Grace at the Intersections - by Rick Rusaw and Eric Swanson, 2006.

Through personal examples and hundreds of heartwarming stories of selfless living, the reader is challenged to move from living a life of dull routine to a life filled with passion and the pursuit of purposeful adventure filled living.

The underlying theme of the book is the life story of the reader and how this relates to God's bigger story. The reader is: encouraged to record his passions, purpose, priorities and values; to examine how they connect with other's stories; to recognize resources to help, with others, write new endings to their stories; and commit to making a difference beyond life here on earth.

The authors encourage the reader to write the "rest of the story" of their own lives by using the questions at the end of each chapter to record personal responses to soul-searching questions that incorporate what they know into action steps for serving others. (taken from Amazon.com review).

- Unfinished Business: Returning the Ministry to the People of God - Greg Ogden, 1991.

This book emphasizes that Martin Luther's Reformation of the Christian church was incomplete - the church must still make ministry by the people and for the people. This volume emphasizes how this can be done. A bit theologically dense but a powerful read.

- Personality Plus - Florence Littauer, 2004.

An excellent resource for those who have taken PLACE and want more information on personality types in action.

- The Purpose Driven Life: What on Earth Am I Here For? (Expanded Edition) - Rick Warren, 2002.

This excellent book discusses five truths to answer this question of why we are here. According to Warren, we exist for the purposes of worship, ministry, evangelism, fellowship and discipleship. He states that in fulfilling these roles on earth, we find and fulfill our purposes. A great guide to living the Christian life successfully and fully.

- S.H.A.P.E.: Finding and Fulfilling Your Unique Purpose for Life - Erik Rees, 2006.

Like the PLACE program, this book presents an examination of a person's personality, spiritual gifts, abilities, passions, and experiences and how they play a role in finding a personal ministry. This book also takes the idea further by getting into how to develop the right God-pleasing attitudes and heart, such as surrendering your personal agenda to God's will. A great tool!

- The Shaping of Things to Come: Innovation and Mission for the 21st-Century Church - Michael Frost and Alan Hirsch, 2003.

Written more from a missionary than an academic perspective, this book redefines how we do church - bringing the concepts of innovation and mission outside the box, and encouraging the reader to use his imagination rather than a prescribed 5-step program to accomplish this intention.

- Simply Strategic Volunteers - Tony Morgan and Tim Stevens, 2005.

Tips on how to handle various situations that come up while working with volunteers - very practical and common sense stuff.

- Ultimate Leadership - J. Townsend

This is a CCN broadcast - see pastor to borrow it - that covers different kinds of leaders and how to be more effective, especially by following a path of growth for the group (having a future orientation).

- The Volunteer Revolution - Unleashing the Power of Everybody - by Bill Hybels

An excellent, motivating book on the role of volunteer ministers in the church - many powerful stories illustrate his point that every member can do ministry.

Websites

- Cloud-Townsend: Solutions for Life

Resource for wide variety of topics including marriage, emotional struggles, leadership, parenting, and more. Many topics covered in a video format.

- Church Volunteer Central

This site, operated by Group Publishing, contains articles on everything from developing team-based ministry to preventing volunteer burn-out. Full use requires a fee.

- Corporation for National and Community Service (dead link) - homepage

This website provides info on grants, tips for working with volunteers, and much more!

- Corporation for National and Community Service - section for churches (dead link)

This website helps volunteer organizations (including church ministries) to get grants, training, and technical assistance to expand their work. Great resource for tips on working with volunteers.

- Corporation for National and Community Service - Wisconsin page (dead link)

Describes grants available for Wisconsin non-profit organizations and more info on volunteering in our state.

- Enduring Truth (dead link)

The website for listening to/purchasing broadcasts on a variety of topics from Pastor Paul Sheppard.

- Energize Inc. - Especially for Leaders of Volunteers

Here is a list of membership associations at provincial, state and local level for professionals who lead volunteer programs.

- Externally Focused Network

Provides resources such as seminars for ministry leaders.

- FASTEN Network

The Faith and Service Technical Education Network (FASTEN) offers informational resources and networking opportunities to faith-based practitioners, private philanthropies, and public administrators who seek to collaborate effectively to renew urban congregations.

Leadership Network fosters church innovation and growth through strategies, programs, tools and resources consistent with our far-reaching mission: to identify, connect and help high-capacity Christian leaders multiply their impact.

- Leadership Training Network

Basically, a search engine on popular topics relevant to leaders in ministry.

- [Learn and Serve America's National Service-Learning Clearinghouse](#)

Learn and Serve America's

- [Vital Churches Institute](#)

A great resource for seminars and other materials centered around equipping pastors and leaders to help the laity become involved in ministry.

- [Walk Thru the Bible](#)

The homepage for Walk Thru the Bible Ministries, a great resource for seminars, books, devotionals, and videos.